The Little Book of
NATURE

By Zack Bush and Laurie Friedman
Illustrated by Sarah Van Evera

DEDICATED TO YOU –
OUR WONDERFUL READER

THIS BOOK BELONGS TO:

_____

Copyright © 2022 Publishing Power, LLC
All Rights Reserved
All inquiries about this book can be sent
to the author at info@thelittlebookof.com
Published in the United States by Publishing Power, LLC
ISBN: 978-1-959141-02-0
For more information, visit our website:
www.BooksByZackAndLaurie.com
Paperback

When you walk outside,
what do you see?

Flowers and trees? Birds and butterflies?
The sun shining in a clear blue sky?
Maybe puffy white clouds in all shapes and sizes?

Did you know that everything you see in the world around you that is not made by people is called **NATURE?**

In **NATURE,** there are so many special things you can enjoy. Not only things that you see, but also things you can hear, smell, touch, and taste.

You can hear . . .

The sound of chirping birds and croaking frogs.

The rustling of leaves as wind blows through trees.
The rush of a flowing river.

You can smell . . .
Blooming flowers
and freshly cut grass.

The aroma of an herb garden.

Salty air at the beach.

You can touch . . .
Soft grass,
smooth stones,
silky flower petals,
and the rough bark of a tree.

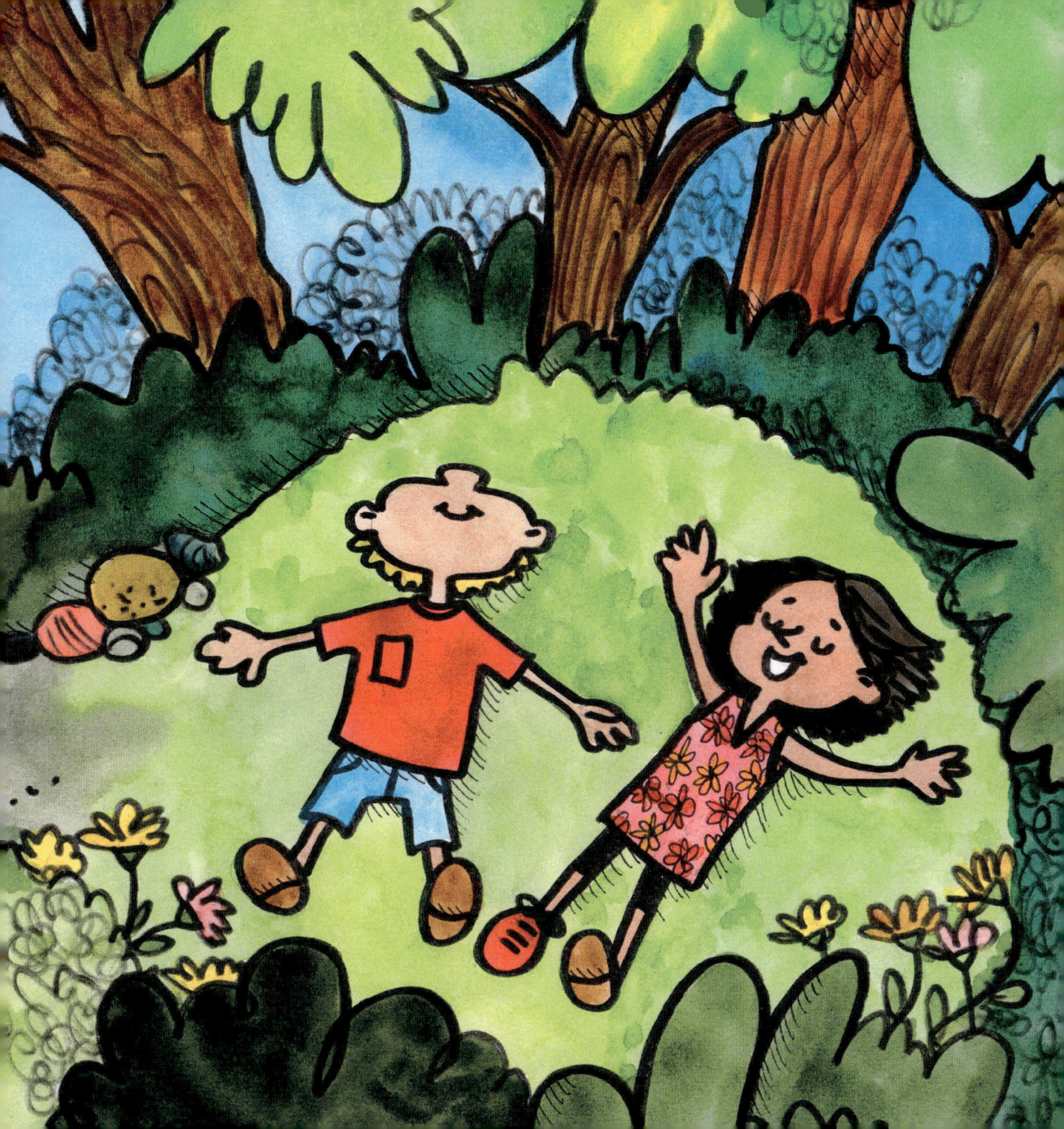

And, of course, many of the foods we eat are grown in **NATURE.** Which ones taste good to you?

BANANAS

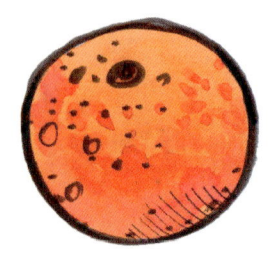

ORANGES

MELONS

TOMATOES

CARROTS

APPLES

CORN	LETTUCE
GRAPES	BROCCOLI
ASPARAGUS	BERRIES

There are lots of fun things you can do outside in **NATURE.**

You can go swimming and boating.

You can take a hike through the woods.

You can build a sandcastle at the beach.

Or have fun jumping in puddles after a rain.

You can plant flowers and study bugs.

You can watch birds or gaze at colorful fish.

One of the most fun times to enjoy **NATURE** is at night.

If you look out your window or go outside with a grown-up, you can see the moon and count the stars in the dark night sky.

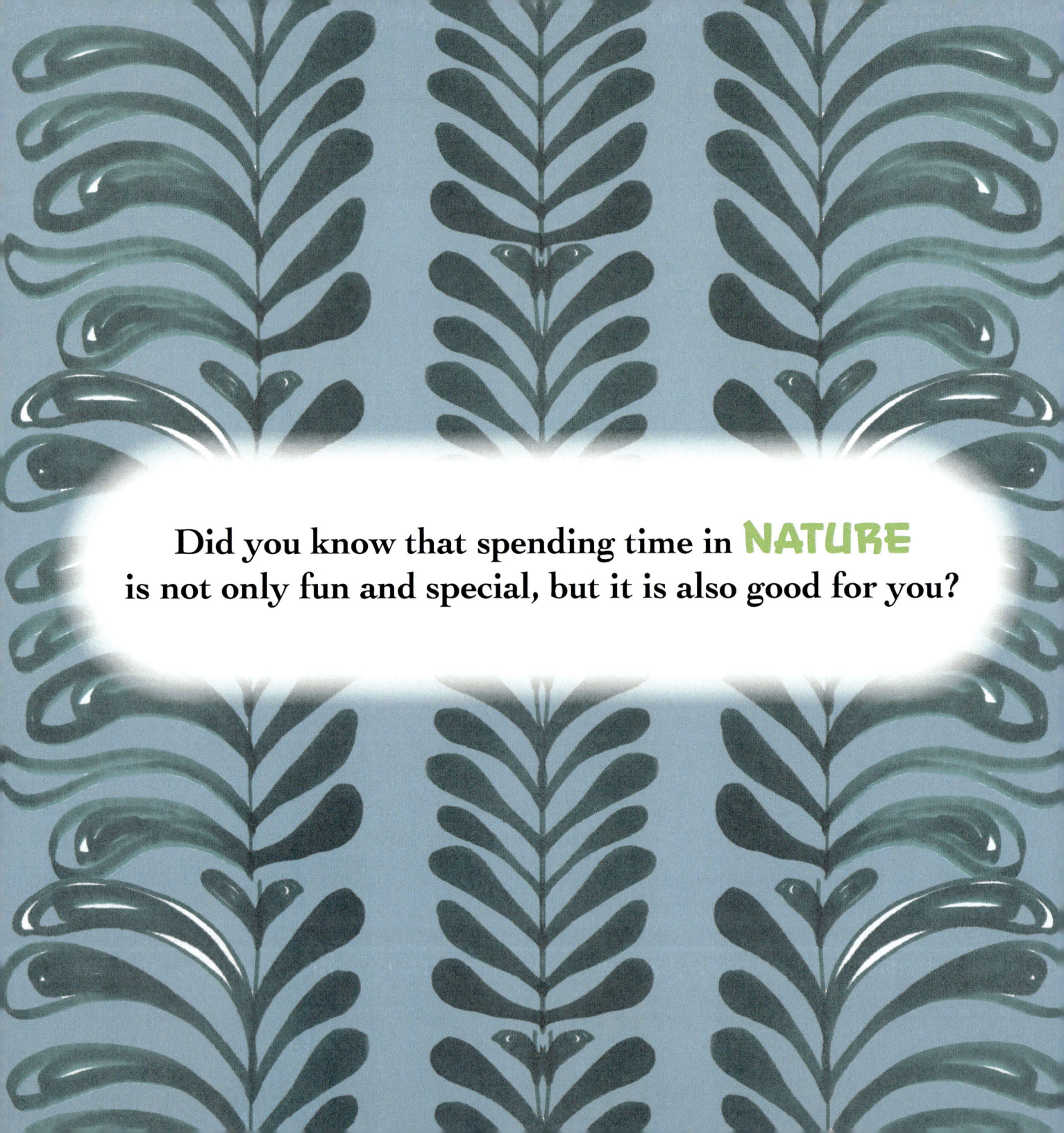

Did you know that spending time in **NATURE** is not only fun and special, but it is also good for you?

When you are outside, you are breathing fresh air.

You are getting vitamins from the sun.

You are giving your body a chance to relax.

It is important to spend time outside, but you can have fun with **NATURE** when you are inside too.

There are so many projects you can do with things that you find in **NATURE.**

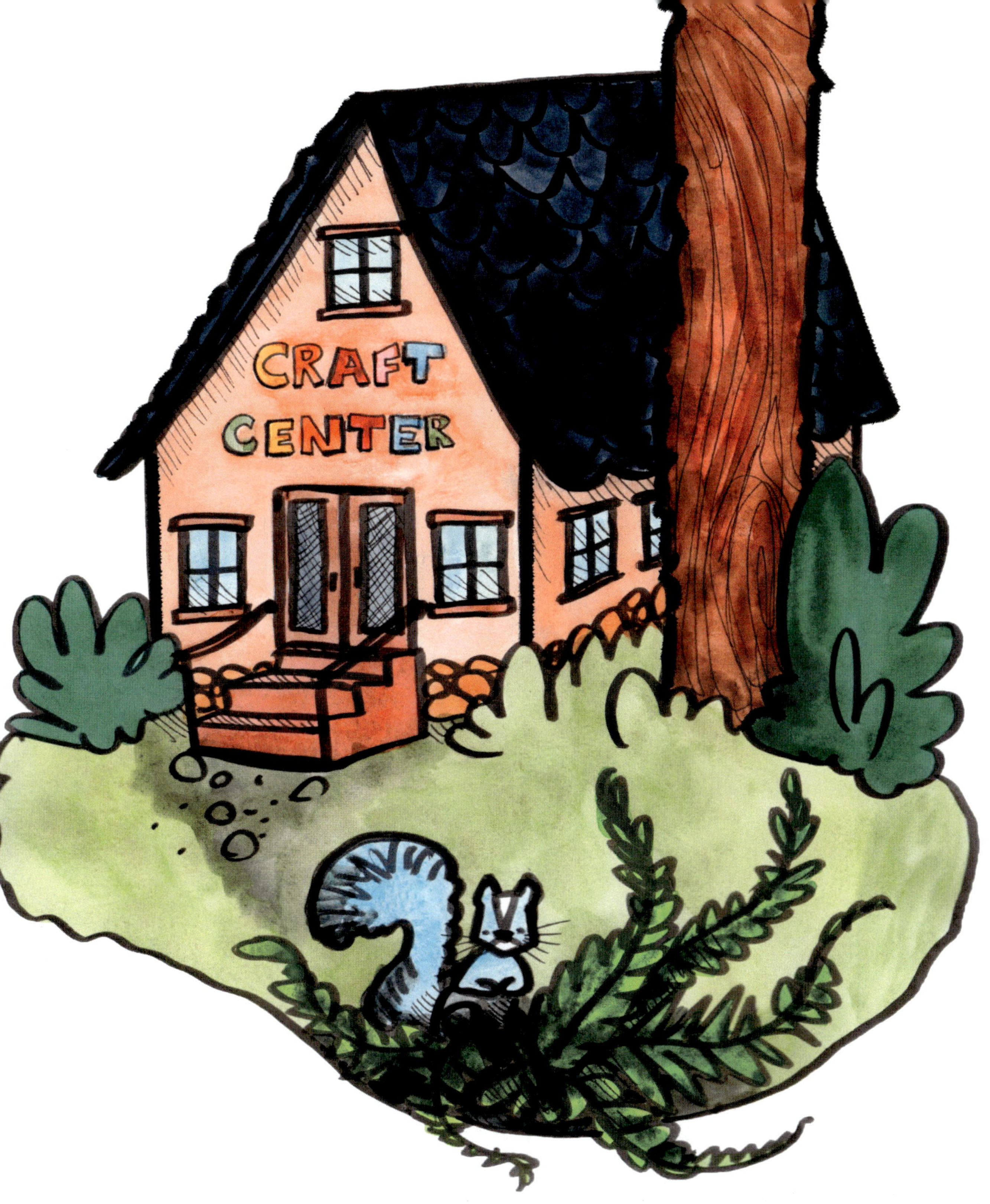
CRAFT
CENTER

You can collect rocks . . .

Then have fun painting them.

You can gather twigs, branches, and leaves . . .

And build all kinds of cool structures.

You can take a special photo...

Then hang it on your wall.

Now you know so many ways to enjoy everything that **NATURE** has to offer.

CONGRATULATIONS!

Here's your NATURE badge.

Just print it out and pin it on.

Go to the website
www.BooksByZackAndLaurie.com
to print out your badges
from the Printables & Activities page.

And if you like this book, please go to
Amazon and leave a kind review.

Other books in the series include:

The Little Book of Camping
The Little Book of Friendship
The Little Book of Kindness
The Little Book of Presidential Elections
The Little Book of Giving
The Little Book of Government
The Little Book of Valentine's Day
The Little Book of Patience
The Little Book of Father's Day
The Little Book of Kindergarten
The Little Book of Halloween
The Little Book of Grandparents
The Little Book of Laughter
The Little Book of Bedtime
The Little Book of Santa Claus
The Little Book of Good Manners
The Little Book of Pets
The Little Book of Creativity
The Little Book of First Grade
The Little Book of Dinosaurs
The Little Book of the Supreme Court
The Little Book of Confidence
The Little Book of Sports
The Little Book of Music

Made in the USA
Monee, IL
29 November 2023